A

TO

Dinas Mawddwy

BY

Charles Ashton.

1893.

J. AND J. GIBSON, ABERYSTWYTH.

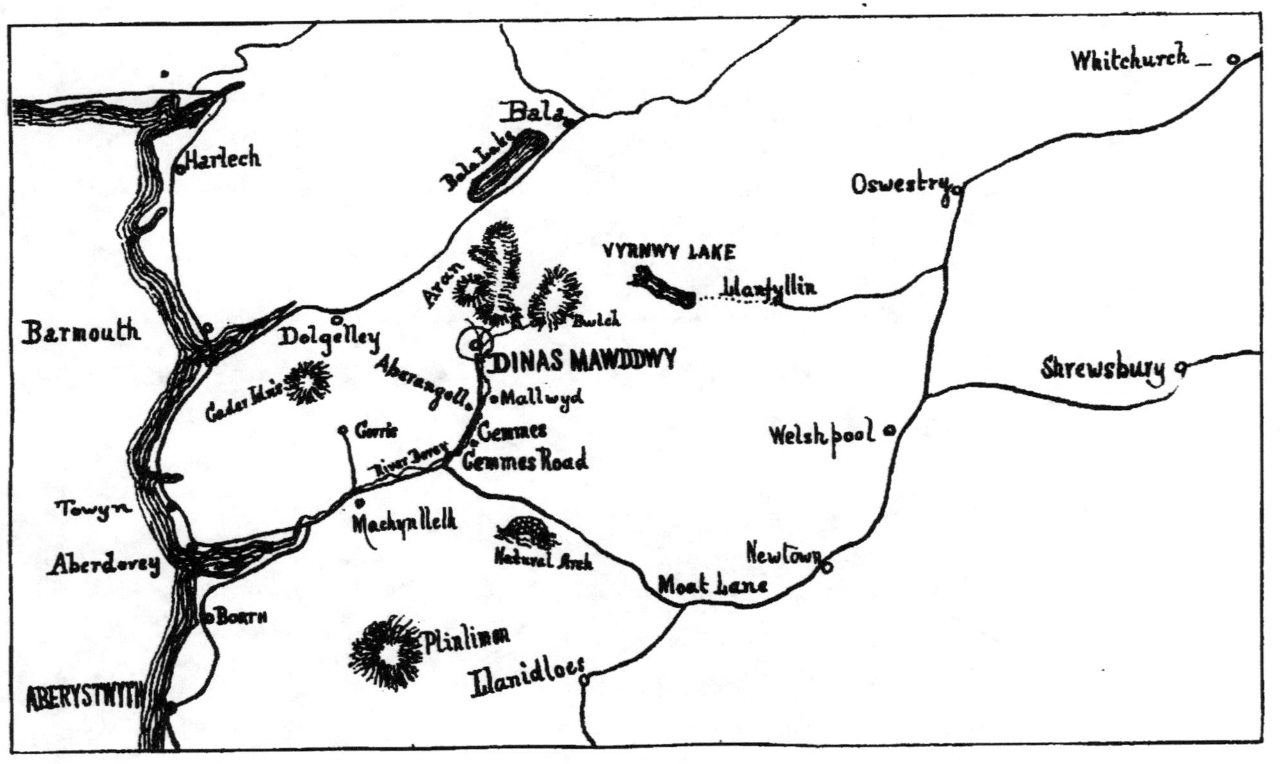

Whitchurch
Bala
Bala Lake
Harlech
Oswestry
VYRNWY LAKE
Aran
Llanfyllin
Barmouth
Dolgelley
Bwlch
DINAS MAWDDWY
Shrewsbury
Aberangell
Cader Idris
Mallwyd
Corris
Cemmes
Welshpool
River Dovey
Cemmes Road
Towyn
Machynlleth
Natural Arch
Newtown
Aberdovey
Moat Lane
Borth
Plinlimon
Llanidloes
ABERYSTWYTH

A WINTER SCENE AT DINAS MAWDDWY.

A

GUIDE

TO

DINAS MAWDDWY

BY

CHARLES ASHTON,

AUTHOR OF

"Bywyd ac Amserau yr Esgob Morgan,"

&c. &c., &c.

PRICE TWOPENCE.

Aberystwyth

PRINTED BY J. & J. GIBSON, "CAMBRIAN NEWS" OFFICE,
MILL STREET.

INDEX.

DINAS MAWDDWY.

As a Health Resort.

To those who delight in elbowing and jostling their way through thick crowds, in being half suffocated by the smoky atmosphere of the manufacturing districts, and in having their ears deafened by the rumbling of traffic and the clanging of machinery, a journey to Dinas Mawddwy would be simply futile. Neither can the place boast of theatres, music halls, dancing saloons, or a zoological garden. And worse even than that, it has no shop windows that would tempt a lady of fashion to slacken her usual pace. Dinas Mawddwy can boast of nothing that gratifies the senses of the lover of art or of fashion. But to those who wish to spend a few weeks, or months, peaceably and quietly in a neighbourhood where nature has been most lavish of her charms and adornments, a visit to Dinas Mawddwy would not be taken in vain. Here they may enjoy mountain walks and mountain air; eat Welsh mutton, fresh butter, and new-laid eggs; and drink fresh milk without running the risk of imbibing chalk and water in mistake. The visitor will have an opportunity to study rustic life among the cheerful and kind-hearted farmers and peasants of the district. He may, if he cares, learn from their lips their folk-lore and traditions; and he will be able to compare them with those of other branches of the Celtic race or with those of his Teutonic or Norman ancestors. If the visit is made in the summer, he will be enchanted by the rich and varied scenery of hill and dale, beautified by covers and woodland, by the bloom of the honey-suckle, the wild rose, and the myriads of wild-ngs that grow in lanes and fields.

Where, and What, is Dinas Mawddwy ?

The village of Dinas Mawddwy is situated in the parish of Mallwyd, on the east side of Merionethshire, and on the borders of Montgomeryshire. It may be reached by travelling on the Cambrian Railways to Cemmes Road Station, where the passenger will have to change for the Mawddwy Railway, which takes him to his destination after pursuing his journey for about seven miles in a northerly direction. The course of the Mawddwy Railway lies through the beautiful Dovey Valley. The traveller in this last stage will have a momentary glance at varied scenery of rich pasture and lofty mountains ; at groups of trees and neat cottages, with the river Dovey rolling by in a meandering form. On arriving at the station, the traveller will imagine himself within a mile of land's end. With his back to the tortuous vale through which the train has just brought him, he finds himself in a small amphitheatre of about half a mile in breadth, enclosed by hills which seem to hide their heads in the clouds. On his left stands the perpendicular hill called Moel Dre', or Moel Dinas, covered by a variegated crop of larch and Scotch firs with different varieties of pines. On his right he finds sloping fields and masses of trees, leading up to a thick plantation, called Cefncoch, at the top. And in front of him, at a distance of about a mile, in strange contrast to the surrounding scenery, stands the steep, barefaced hill called Moel Benddin, with the entrance to the Cerist valley bashfully showing itself between the plantations on the left side of it, and the Cowarch valley, more emboldened, coming to view, in the form of a scooped ravine, on the right of it.

The traveller may take rooms either at the Buckley Arms Hotel, which is within one minutes' walk from the station ; the Peniarth Arms Hotel, Mallwyd, about a mile in the opposite direction ; at one of the two inns—the Red Lion and Nag's Head—in the village of Dinas; or, again, if he likes it better, he may take private lodgings at Dinas, Minllyn, or in cottages situated in the surrounding neighbourhood.

We have already more than implied that Dinas Mawddwy is a village; and we may call it a very small village, as the number of its adult inhabitants does not exceed one hundred. However, the inhabitants take it almost as an insult if the place is called anything but a *town*, which word they invariably use. It is situated to the north of the station, and it may be reached in about 7 minutes. It is the headquarters of the two parishes—Mallwyd and Llanymawddwy; the inhabitants of which are mostly employed in agricultural pursuits. It is true there are a few slate and slab quarries in the neighbourhood, one at Minllyn, near the Railway Station; and three at some distance from Aberangell Station, called Maesygamdda, Gartheiniog, and Hendreddu; and here we may mention that the managers invariably treat visitors with the greatest courtesy, by affording facilities for inspection of the quarries. But Dinas Mawddwy, in days long gone by, was something superior to a town; it was a city. The meaning of *Mawddwy* has never been explained to our satisfaction; but it is almost needless to say that *Dinas* is the Welsh word for *city* or *stronghold*. And two spots are pointed out on which, according to tradition, there stood British fortifications. One is on the summit of Moel Benddin, to which we shall refer again; and the other is on the field between the Buckley Arms Hotel and the Minllyn school-room. The field we refer to is called Cae'r-bryn. On the south-west corner of it there is a considerable depression, which is believed to represent where the dungeon was situated. However, not a stone is to be found here now; but we have been informed by persons, now about 60 years of age, that their grandfathers had seen stones there. There is also a tradition that there was a subterranean passage from this fortress running towards the river—but to where, we are not told. Another tradition states that this castle was once attacked by the Romans from Cefncoch, above Gloddfa

Goch. About 20 years ago an urn, containing ashes, was found near the Minllyn Sheds.

An Ancient Borough.

From mediæval times up to the year 1886, Dinas Mawddwy was a borough; and could boast of its mayor, its recorder, and its burgesses. The mayor, in olden times, was a justice of the peace, and possessed the power of trying offenders within the borough; but his only mode of punishment consisted in ordering his prisoners to the "*veg vawr*"—or great fetter—or the stocks, but not in the county gaol, for incarceration. He sat with the county magistrates to grant licenses to public-houses, which privilege was subsequently altered to signing the licences and sending them to the Dolgelley magistrates to be confirmed; however, even that practice has been discontinued since the passing of the Licensing Act, 1872. And the corporation, with its double-necked spread eagle for its seal and arms, was abolished, with many other useless boroughs, by an Act of Parliament. We may mention that no charter of incorporation is known; but there is a charter purported to have been granted by James I. giving to the Lord of the Manor certain fairs to be held within the borough. The number of fairs, from time immemorial, were five—Friday before Palm Sunday, June 2, Sept. 10, Oct. 18, and Nov. 14. Two additional fairs were fixed in 1893, viz., the Tuesday before the first Wednesday in February, and October 2nd. The Dinas Mawddwy fairs up to the time when railways were constructed over the country were most popular, especially so the June fair--called "Ffair Dinas yr Ha'." The place being central, buyers and sellers met here from all parts; and the streets, highways, and the common called Dolybont—near the Red Lion—were literally swarmed with cattle and horses. On the day after the fair, the cattle were provided with iron shoes to enable them to walk to the English markets. The fairs are still held, but have dwindled into insignificance compared with what they were in the good old times.

The Court Leet.

This Court is held twice a year at the Buckley Arms Hotel, usually in May and November. The following is a copy of the official notice for the Court held in November, 1891 :—

MANOR OF MAWDDWY.

NOTICE IS HEREBY GIVEN that the COURT LEET, Court Baron, and View of Frankpledge of and for the above Manor, and for the City and Borough of Dinas Mawddwy, for Michaelmas, 1891, will be held at the Buckley Arms Hotel, Dinas Mawddwy, on Thursday, the 19th day of November next, at One o'clock in the Afternoon, where and when all Jurors, Constables, Homagers, and others who owe suit and service are required to attend.

W. R. DAVIES,
Steward.

Dolgelley, Oct. 31st, 1891.

The Court is presided over by the Steward of the Manor, which office is now, and for some years past, held by Mr. W. R. Davies, Solicitor, Dolgelley. Another officer of the Court is Mr. David Lloyd, who was appointed Bailiff of the Manor in 1889 ; his father, also of the same name, had held the office for fifty-three years. The Manor of Mawddwy includes the whole of the parishes of Mallwyd and Llanymawddwy (except the township of Caereinion Fechan in the former), over which the jurisdiction of the Court extends. We do not know who was the first Lord of the Manor; but we are informed that Bleddyn ab Cynvyn—who flourished in the eleventh century—was the prince of Powys and the Lord of Mawddwy. The lordship was for some centuries since in the possession of the Myttons of Halston, the last of whom that held it being the noted "Jack" Mytton. After his time it passed through purchase into the possession of a Mr. Bird ; and subsequently from him to the present Lord of the Manor—Sir Edmund Buckley, Bart.—whose country seat is *The Plâs*, situated at the north end of Dinas.

The Fishing.

As it is probable that our visitors care more for the fishing, and the scenery the place affords, than for its history and antiquities, we will proceed. The fishing is by no means the least attractive feature of the neighbourhood. The Dovey is noted for its salmon, sewin, and trout ; and the angler frequently returns with a good basket. The trout season opens on February 1st, and closes September 30th; and the salmon season is open from May 1st to November 30th. Visitors staying at the Buckley Arms Hotel, and the Peniarth Arms Hotel, Mallwyd, have the privilege of going over certain lands, and where they may also obtain licenses to fish for salmon and sewin, on paying 10s. for the season, 5s. per month, 2s. 6d. per week, and 1s. per diem. Taking for granted that the disciples of Isaak Walton may wish to vary their favourite pastime by the contemplation of some beautiful scenery, we will just point out a few chosen walks and excursions.

Moel Dre', or Moel Dinas,

on the west side of the village, is well worth an ascent for the sake of the view it affords of The Plâs and the village. This pine-covered hill is about 1,400 feet high; and to attempt to climb its almost perpendicular side would prove very difficult. Perhaps the easiest ascent commences through the gate which is situated near a superannuated toll-bar, between the Buckley Arms Hotel and Dinas. This road may be followed till the Minllyn Quarry is reached; the proprietors of which—the Messrs. Bullock—would be most happy to show visitors the manufacturing sheds and workings. After leaving the quarry we keep to the right. The prospect at the top, to the west and the north, is rather confined by the surrounding hills; but a splendid view is obtained of the Dinas valley and its branches. If the traveller has time at his disposal he may visit either Maesglasau, to the north; or Aberangell, to the south. Whichever of these two roads he may take, he will, according to place-names, traverse through grounds that were once the centres of ecclesiastical activity.

Maesglasau.

By following the ridge northwards, he will come to a narrow ledge, being the top of a precipice forming the upper end of a dingle. When he gets to the bottom of this precipice he will stumble across the remains of Bwlch-y-siglen

Gold Mine. This mine was opened about 40 years ago, and was worked for several years with two results. One was that more gold was put in than got out; and the other, that hundreds of very fine fish were killed. Quicksilver was used so freely and injudiciously, in attempting to extract the gold, that pilferers made a lot of money by collecting it in the brook—one person having collected about 16lbs. of it. Descending this dingle in the direction of the Dolgelley road, we leave Maesglasau—now an uninhabited farmhouse—to the right. Maesglasau, or Maesglassrey, has been translated by some into "the field of the cloisters," which, if correct, denotes its ecclesiastical origin. This theory is slightly confirmed by the dingle on the left being called Cwm-yr-Eglwys. However, we know that Maesglasau was the birth-place of Hugh Jones, the Welsh hymnologist, who died during the first quarter of the present century. Below Maesglasau, on the Cwm-yr-Eglwys side of the valley, is a farm-house called Ty'nybraich, occupied by Mr. Robert Evan Jones, a most respected freeholder, who, through a long line of ancestors, can trace his pedigree to one Llywelyn Griffith ap Gethin, the owner and occupier of the place in the year 1012. The road from Ty'nybraich joins the Dolgelley road through a gate called "Llidiart Maes-y-llys" (the Gate of the Court field). The origin of the name is unknown to us; and our nearest guess is, that one of the adjoining fields was the scene of a trial concerning landed property, held in accordance with the old Welsh laws of Howel the Good.

Cerist Mill

is an antiquated looking building, worthy of the artist's brush or pencil, and may be reached by taking the Dolgelley road for about a hundred yards from Llidiart Maes-y-llys, where we take a turn to the right. The old mill-house presents quite a picturesque appearance from the common on the opposite side of the Cerist brook.

Aberangell.

If our traveller prefers it, instead of returning from the

top of Moel Dre' by Maesglasau, he may deviate to the left, passing the farmhouse and quarry called Cae'r Batty—supposed to mean the Abbot's Field—making straight for Blaenycwm, also the site of a former ecclesiastical building; and he will follow the wooded dingle of Cwm Du until he reaches Abermynach (the confluence of the Monk), where the little brook that kept his company joins another called the Mynach. Here he enters a tramway employed to carry slabs from the quarry, which he may visit by turning on the right. Following the tramway for about a mile and a half, leaving at some distance on the left the beautiful residence of Cwmllecoediog, belonging to Frederick Walton, Esq., he finds Gartheiniog quarry just in front of him on the right. Maesygamdda quarry may be reached by following the tramway to the right from Gartheiniog; and Hendreddu by following the tramway from Gartheiniog to the left. We had almost forgotten to mention the splendid and expansive scenery that may be obtained from the top of Maesygamdda sheep-walk—Esgair-wen. Here, standing in Merionethshire, we have a glimpse of parts of the counties of Salop, Montgomery, Radnor, Brecknock, Cardigan, Denbigh, and Carnarvon; and the summits of Snowdon, Cader Idris, Aran Mawddwy, Berwyn, and Plynlymon, may be seen. Retracing our steps past Abermynach, we come in a few minutes to the small village of Aberangell. And if we find we have some time to wait for our train, we may visit the site of a traditional church called Llandybo, which we reach by climbing the hill at the back of Aberangell Terrace. The site is quite at the northern corner of the hill, but there are no ruins. However, an outline of a building may be clearly discerned; and tradition insists that there was a church here, but forgets to say when, or to give any other particulars. A three miles ride in the train will bring us from Aberangell to Dinas Mawddwy.

From Dinas to Dolgelley

(10 miles by road) would be an excursion worth making. The road winds beneath Moel Dinas, having, for nearly a

mile, The Plâs grounds on the right. Continuing along our road, we keep high up on the side of the valley, with Moel Benddin blocking our path behind, and about three miles out reach the foot of Bwlchoerddrws (the Pass of the Cold Door). The ascent is steep, but the view in front is fine. We may mention here that the top of this pass is pointed out as one of the three places where the most influential and powerful individuals of certain districts met, and entered into a solemn compact for enforcing the strict dispensation of justice for all wrongs done prior and subsequent to the so-called rebellion of Owain Glyndwr, about the beginning of the fifteenth century, whereby each person who had been deprived of property was to have it restored to him without lawsuit; and various regulations for restoring the government of the country were resolved upon. Continuing our course, we notice to our left the peak of Y Waun Oer (2,107 feet); and on reaching the Dolgelley head of the pass, we see that district opening out in front. The range of Cader Idris, with its numerous nodding summits, comes gradually and grandly into sight; and the pass of Craig-y-llam, with that ominous-looking rock itself, opens to the left. Far away in front, a part of the river Wnion, near Bontddu, appears like a small lake, surrounded by a lovely vale which is covered with trees and pretty houses. At the Dolgelley foot of the Pass, after a long and rough, but gradual, descent, "Cross Foxes"—the inn so famous for the favourite ascent of Cader Idris—is reached. Its name, by the way, has been changed to "Caerynwch Arms," from the neighbouring estate of Caerynwch. The road forks here; that to the left runs to Tal-yllyn and Corris. To Dolgelley, we can take our choice of three ways:—(1) by taking the old road, which commands a fine view of the valley; or (2) by taking the high road, which is about a mile longer; or (3) by a slight detour, to the right, from the high road we may continue our journey viâ the Torrent walk, on the Caerynwch estate. This favourite tourist's paradise is exquisitely lovely; although, it may be, too fervent admirers have over-rated its beauty to the exclusion of quite as beautiful places of the same description.

The quaint old town of Dolgelley dozes all the year round under the shadow of Mynydd Moel, one of the peaks of Cader. Historically, it is interesting as connected with Owain Glyndwr and his traditional parliament. But as a town it is remarkable for nothing but its quaintness and the irregular way in which its houses are scattered about. The church, although a picturesque feature in the general view of the town. is a very unlovely building, dating from the early years of this century, and containing some very ugly stained-glass windows. But, if unattractive in point of general interest, Dolgelley is a magnificent centre for holiday-makers; and such excursions as the ascent of Cader Idris, the Precipice and Torrent Walks, and a drive to the Gwynfynydd Gold Mines in the Ganllwyd valley, or a trip of 10 miles by train to Barmouth, amply repay a visit of some duration. Visitors to Dolgelley, who wish to spend a few hours at Barmouth, may return to Dinas Mawddwy by a late train on the same day, viâ Cemmes Road.

Talyllyn Lake and Corris.

Visitors wishing to make an excursion from Dinas to these places may walk or drive along the Dolgelley road as far as Cross Foxes; then turning to the left and continuing as far as Bwlch-llyn-bach (pass of the little pool) they will see Talyllyn Lake in the valley far below. This pass is a narrow ravine, bounded on the right by a shoulder of Cader; and on the left by the fearful precipice of Craig-y-llam (Rock of the leap), where, it is said, felons in ancient times were compelled to leap into certain death. The Pass is also noted for its Llyn Bach (Little Pool), which tradition asserts has no bottom, as well as for the "Three Pebbles," or huge masses of rock, that lie near it. As for the "pebbles," tradition tells us that the giant Idris one day felt something in his shoe hurting him, so he pulled it off and shook out the three boulders, the largest of which is *only* about 24 feet long, 18 feet broad, and 12 feet high. We are not informed who was Idris's shoemaker, nor what he paid for his shoes. Ascending the pass, the road branches into two after passing Minffordd farm; the one to the left leading to Corris, and the one to the right to Talyllyn. This latter road branches off again at the end of the lake, so that we may take either side of it. The lake, which is celebrated for its trout, is about a mile long and a quarter of a mile wide; and at the bottom of it stands Ty'nycornel Hotel, Penybont Inn, the parish church, and three or four houses. Our traveller now, being 12 miles from Dinas, may return by the way of Corris (3½ miles) and hence by train, changing at Machynlleth and Cemmes Road.

Moel Benddin (1,700 FEET).

The tourist might spend half a day pleasantly by ascending this hill, which commands a more expansive view than Moel Dinas. To avoid the extreme labour of climbing the steep ascent above Ty'nypwll, at the south end of it, we may take the Dolgelley road as far as Mynogau farm, two miles from Dinas. Passing this farm, we come to the Graig-wen Lead Mine, which has not been worked for many years. This Mine is interesting, inasmuch as it is one of those mines opened by the Romans; but a great deal of money has been spent on it since their departure. Leaving the Mine, we make as straight as we can for the top. After reaching the elevation, we bear to the right till we come to the south end of the hill. There, in a small hollow, according to tradition, is the site of a British fortification. But as might be expected, only very faint traces are discernible. Local philologists are not quite agreed as to the proper name of the hill. It is invariably called Moel Benddin, which means, according to some, a hill with a castle on the top—*din* from the Latin *dinum*, signifying a city or a fortified place. Others think that Moel Benddin is a corruption of the word Moel Beddau (Hill of the Graves); and they fortify their contention by the tradition that graves and sepulchral urns were found in making the road from Dinas to Abercowarch, just where Maesbenddin farm now stands. But independent of the question of the British fortress, the climber will be well rewarded by most charming scenery. He will obtain a splendid view of the Cerist valley on his right; to the south lies the whole length of the Dovey valley, with Dinas at the top, and the mountain of Plynlimon (2,623 feet) with its attendant hills forming the background far in the south. Turning to the left, we see the little village of Abercowarch nestling quietly at the entrance to the Llanymawddwy valley; and more to the left still lies the Cowarch valley, with the Aran showing its lofty head in the distance. The general effect of the scenery is considerably enhanced by observing the groups of cottages and farm-houses which are scattered in the villages beneath. The cultivated fields appear like so many gardens, where the peasants are busied in gathering in the harvest, and when the stillnes of a balmy afternoon is only broken by their merry laugh and an occasional snatch at one of the old airs which have made Wales so dear to the musical student. For variety sake, we may, if we have hobnailed boots, make our descent to the Cowarch valley, where a famous witch of the name of Bessie Richards lived long, long ago. This old hag was a terror to the whole neighbourhood. Those who had the courage to refuse her importunities were soon made the victims of her craft. A neighbouring farmer, in the capacity of a churchwarden, had once offended her; and, in less than three minutes, his sheep were rolling down the Cowarch rock in great numbers. He wisely called after the witch, made his peace with her, and so the remainder of his flock were saved. It appears that Bessie practised the black art, not only for the sake of vengeance but also to gratify a mere whim. Going one day to Llanymawddwy, some boys asked her to cause the ox and the horse, which were yoked to a plough in a field on Coedcae farm, to fall flat on the ground. The horse fell immediately, and the ox went on its knees She explained that she was unable to make the ox fall lower than the knees, because it was equipped with a yoke collar made of mountain ash. We mention this as an useful charm against witchcraft, which the reader is quite at liberty to use without paying us any additional fee for the information. But there came an end to Bessie's witching career. There came to the neighbourhood a skilful conjuror, known as Dick Smot. When his fame spread about, he was requested to do away with the witch. Soon after, Bessie began to run about like a mad woman along the valley, and, at last, she was seen, transformed into a wisp of withered fern, and was blown by a sudden gust of wind in the direction of Mallwyd. She never re-appeared at Cowarch; but her body was shortly afterwards discovered in the weir above Mallwyd bridge. Leaving Bessie Richards to her fate, we follow the narrow lane at the foot of the hill till we get to the high road that leads us back to Dinas.

The Ascent of Aran.

HEIGHT 2,972 FEET.

Aran Mawddwy, next to Snowdon, is the highest mountain in Wales; and probably commands the best view of any, from its very central position. With its neighbour, Aran Benllyn, it may be easily ascended from many points. The least difficult, and at the same time the most uninteresting ascent, is that from Drwsynant, midway between Dolgelley and Bala. Another ascent is from Llanuwchllyn, at the top of Bala Lake. But, by far, the most picturesque and varied ascent is that from Dinas Mawddwy. The distance is not more than seven miles; and the time taken by an ordinary walker need not exceed three hours. Starting from Dinas along the Llanymawddwy road, we cross the little stream Cerist, and soon arrive at Abercowarch, skirting on the way the slopes of Moel Benddin. Abercowarch is a charming little hamlet, at the junction of the Cowarch and the Dovey; and there is no prettier spot in the neighbourhood than the bridge and the little waterfall just above it. On our right, just before we enter the bridge, a few paces from the road, stands the, now uninhabited, old farm house called Penybont, once the abode of Gaynor Fychan, who, on September 16th, 1686, died at the fine old age of 140 years; and that without ever having been further than ten miles from the house in which she was born. Octogenarians are not uncommon in the Mawddwy district, and that speaks well for its salubrity; but of all our ancestors, Gaynor Fychan, probably, was the only one in modern times that could have successfully competed with the post-diluvian patriarchs. We may also mention that it was at this village of Abercowarch that George Borrow, as he tells us in his "Wild Wales," jumped half a yard in the air under the false impression that it was the birth-place of the Rev. Ellis Wynne, the author of the "Visions of the Sleeping Bard," However, Abercowarch cannot boast of such an honour.

At Abercowarch we leave the Llanymawddwy road, and, taking a lane to the left, find ourselves in Cwm Cowarch, where we have paid a former visit, as the reader may recollect, to call upon the witch Bessie Richards. We are now on the other side of that deep valley, which is from a quarter to half-a-mile wide, studded with little farms, and watered by the Cowarch brook, which runs merrily along the deep, trough-like bottom. On our right is Moel Cowarch; on our left Moel Benddin; and in front, as a huge sign of "No Thoroughfare"—in spite of which, however, we will persevere with our walk—is the strange crag, Craig Cowarch, with its tremendous precipices. There is no more romantic valley than this in all North Wales, especially if seen at early morning or sunset. About a mile from Abercowarch, we pass the opening of the small valley known as Cwm Terwyn; and, in another mile, having passed on the way two contiguous chapels bearing the names of Tarsus and Bethlehem, we, with a strange disregard for geography, make our way through the fine, level common called Fawnog Fawr, to the upper end of the valley.

Of course, a fine summer day is absolutely imperative for this excursion. If possible, the start should be made in the early forenoon, so as to see Cwm Cowarch when the morning mists are just clearing away. A mid-day rest might be taken at the disused lead mines at the end of the valley—a place intended by Nature for a picnic. If the day continues fine, we proceed by making for Hen Gwm, the valley facing us at Blaencowarch farm, down which runs a small stream. Following either the right or left bank—it makes but little difference—we ascend. Here it is rather steep and uninteresting; but, once at the head of the valley, our climbing is over; and we are on the ridge of

Aran. Care must be taken to avoid the bogs. Aran is one vast sponge; and, although there are no dangerous morasses, what there are cannot but be unpleasant. Keeping along the ridge, with the mountains about Barmouth and Harlech standing out clearly to our left, we gradually ascend until the ground becomes firmer, and more rocky. At last, after climbing a rock-strewn slope, we arrive at the huge cairn forming the summit, which is 2,972 feet above sea-level.

The view is superb. Sheer beneath our feet, to the east and south-east, descend the precipices of Aran, with Craiglyn Dovey lake in the bare-looking valley below, from which we see the infant Dovey running towards the Dinas and Bala road. Beyond are the Berwyn mountains; and, further still, the whole plain of Shropshire, with the Wrekin and Breidden distinctly visible. Moving towards the left, we see the road winding over Bwlchygroes, the wildest pass in Wales; and, in the background, the highest summits of the Berwyns. Then, far away, the Clwydian hills—Moel Fammau marked by its pillars; and, nearer us, the foot of Bala Lake, beyond which is the huge mass of Arrenig Fawr, about ten miles away, with Arrenig Fach to the right, shutting the Festiniog country and the Migneint range from us. Then, in the distance, is Snowdon itself, with its attendant peaks—the Glyders and Lliwedd being most easily distinguishable. In the immediate foreground is the wild mountain district about Trawsfynydd, with the black rock of Castell Carn Dochan standing as a sentinel; and two miles away, the Cairn on Aran Benllyn. Further to our left is the peninsula of Lleyn, with Yr Eifl standing out conspicuously, and Moel Hebog between it and Snowdon. Then follow the Merionethshire mountains in order—Rhinog Fawr and Rhinog Fach, with Drws Ardudwy between, like a huge V.; then Llethr, Diphwys and the Llawllech range; the Mawddach estuary; Moel Orthrwm and Moel Cynwch, where runs the Precipice Walk; and the Rhobell Fawr. On the opposite side of the valley of the Wnion, the whole range of Cader Idris—Mynydd Moel and Penygader—being very noticeable. At the foot of the slope of the Aran is Drwsynant, being the head of the valleys of the Wnion and the Dee. Further to the left, opens the pass of Craig-y-llam (or Bwlchllyn-bach), leading to Talyllyn. Then come the Dinas mountains, with Craig Cowarch peeping out in the foreground; and in the distance, Plynlymon, until we come round again to our starting point.

A very pleasant two miles walk along the top of the fantastic precipices brings us to the sister-peak of Aran Benllyn, which commands a good view of Bala Lake, with Bala at the head; and the Vale of Edeirnion beyond, through which flows the sacred Dee. And from the slopes, a glimpse may be obtained of Lake Vyrnwy—the Liverpool reservoir.

The ordinary mountain climber will probably be content with Aran Mawddwy, and return the way he came; unless he prefers to descend to Drwsynant, and occupy about three hours in the long, but lovely, railway journey by way of Dolgelley, Barmouth Junction, and Cemmes Road, back to Dinas. But an excellent plan for climbers of fair walking abilities is to proceed to Aran Benllyn, and descend into the valley below, via Llyn Lliwbran, a good trout lake. Here he will find a path, which will bring him into the road from Bala to Dinas—about two miles from Llanuwchllyn and eleven miles from Dinas. Having obtained refreshment at one of the neighbouring farm-houses, he will proceed upon what is, without exception, the most magnificent walk in Wales.

We ascend out of the hedge-bordered lanes into a wilder and more rugged district. Soon, Cwm Croes cleanly sweeps away on our right into the bosom of Aran, whose peaks stand out sharp and clear; and the road gets steeper as we advance. At one point—Craig Ddrwg—we have, on our left, a great over-hanging crag, while, to our right are great sloping precipices of shale—a typical mountain path. A milestone soon proclaims that we are half-way between Bala and Dinas; and, about half a mile beyond, we arrive at the top of the pass—BWLCHYGROES (the pass of the Cross), the highest road in Wales, about 2,000 feet above the level of the sea. The name of the pass is derived from a cross which once stood there to remind travellers of the dangers they had passed before arriving at the top, in a time when roads were almost unknown; and when the Mawddwy banditti (Gwylliaid Cochion Mawddwy) made mountain travelling perilous in the extreme. The scene is panoramic. We look down on the tops of the surrounding mountains, and seem to be almost as high as the neighbouring Arans. Behind us, Arrenig blocks our view, like a huge wedge. To its right stands Moel Hebog, which is sometimes falsely pointed out as Snowdon. The most bigoted Alpine enthusiast would find it difficult to mention a more sublime or awe-inspiring scene, especially at sunset. The feeling is akin to that which we experience when looking from a tall church-tower—a sense of novelty, tempered with fear and reverence for the Creating Hand.

The descent along a valley bordered on one side by steep scaurs, which make the eye dizzy, is most impressive. The road improves as we descend; and, at last, we come round a very steep curve into the Dovey valley. To our left, opens Cwm Llaethnant, with Aran visible at its head, and the Dovey falling down its slope. Behind us, the imposing double peak, known as Tap Nyth yr Eryr—once famous, as its name implies, for its eagles' nests—guards the pass we have just crossed. The country now becomes rural, and we pass between pretty hedge-rows; with the river rippling along the valley, as yet but a mere stream. Three miles from the top of Bwlchygroes, passing Y Bryn—the country seat of Sir William Roberts—on our left, we enter the village of Llanymawddwy, by crossing the brook Pumrhyd. The valley gets more beautiful as we approach Dinas. About half way to our destination we pass, in pretty grounds to the right, Ty'n-y-Coed—a castellated residence belonging to W. A. Copinger, Esq., of Manchester. A short mile further, we reach Abercowarch again, and so regain our original road. This interesting excursion, allowing for frequent rests on the ascent, would not take more than 12 hours for a walker of average abilities. And the consciousness of having obtained enjoyment of the highest order, combined with healthy exercise, more than compensates for a weary body and tired feet. The sensible traveller who delights to mingle intellectual with muscular pleasures, should take with him a copy of the "Gossiping Guide to Wales"—the prince of North Wales guide books—published by Messrs Woodall, Minshall & Co., Oswestry.

Llanymawddwy.

This little village—4 miles from Dinas—deserves more notice than we could afford on our return from the Arans. The village can only boast of a few poor, but antiquated, looking houses, one public house, the Rectory, the Parish Church, and an Independent Chapel. Just before we enter the village, stands a neat little cottage called Cilwern, and here we should apply to Mr Thomas Davies for the necessary permission to visit the "Torrent Walk" on the estate of Sir William Roberts, who kindly allows this privilege to visitors for the mere asking for it. We trust it is unnecessary to ask visitors to abstain from removing or damaging the ferns and shrubs, which render the walk so beautiful. The Torrent Walk commences at the white gate on the left, just at the end of the new bridge over the Pumrhyd brook. Following the path, on which seats are provided at convenient distances, we enter a deep glen shaded by a fine plantation. Proceeding for a short distance, with the Pumrhyd on our left, warbling pleasantly her salutations to the pretty little cascades beneath our feet, whilst the slope on our right—covered with moss, heather, and wildings—is one glowing mass of colour, we arrive at a spot where an exaggerated description would be impossible. Here we find a magnificent waterfall about 80 feet high. Then, we may either cross a wooden bridge to the other side, making our way back to the road; or we may follow the path from the fall for Pencareg-y-Llan, which commands a fine view of the valley. Pursuing our journey we reach the disused lead mine at Blaen Cwm Dynewid; and a little further we are rewarded by the sight of another waterfall, which is truly majestic. Again, if we choose, we may continue our walk and ascend the Aran. But if not, after satiating our vision, if possible, with the charms of this most interesting of walks, to which our pen is quite unable to do justice, we can—with a good appetite—

adjourn to the village public-house, the Sun Inn, for refreshments. Judging from the names of the few houses, we might conclude that most of them at one time in their history had been kept as public houses. For instance we have here the Bull Mawr, Bull Bach, the Crown, and the Boot—names usually dedicated to Bacchus—as well as the Credit and Ty-uchaf, all kept as public houses by our forefathers. Such a number of public houses in such a small place must have been more than enough to disencourage the Sir Wilfred Lawson of those days. However, when the Rev Richard Warner, of Bath, visited the place in the year 1798, he only mentions one public house, but omits the name of it. He, and his friends, had here some "tolerable beer and admirable bread and cheese." But Mr Warner was not partial to Welsh public houses. He brought the charge of keeping short measures against Welsh landlords in general, and against the landlady at Llanymawddwy in particular. "The pint," he says, "as we found by accurately measuring it, contained little more than half an English one, and the quart was equally under the legal size." Had Mr Warner lived now, he would perceive no difference in this respect between Llanymawddwy and Bath.

Llanymawddwy Church and St. Tydecho.

Laying aside such profane things as public-house measures, it behoves us to mention that the church is said to have been founded in the sixth century. Probably the first building as well as some of the succeeding ones were simply wooden structures plastered with clay or mud. At any rate, the present edifice, which cannot lay claim to much architectural pretensions, though clean and neat in appearance, was restored in 1687, and again in 1854. The church is dedicated to Tydecho, one of the great band of Armorican saints which flooded this country in the sixth century. There is a tradition, that previous to erecting a church here, an attempt was made to build one in the Cowarch valley, which is in the same parish. The site selected is situated by a house called Terwyn, which we passed the other day on our way to Aran. The tradition goes on to state that the stones laid down by the masons during the day were removed by some supernatural power during the súcceeding night. We are not told what objections the invisible architect had against this spot, nor by what means he made known the particular site which he had fixed upon. But eventually the workmen transferred their labours to the place where the present edifice stands. However, we may tell visitors that they are by no means compelled to believe the tradition, which seems to be also connected with Llangar Church, near Corwen. Between the Church and the Rectory stands a very fine yew tree, measuring 24 feet 6 inches at the base. Among the former rectors we may mention the name of Canon D. Silvan Evans, B.D.,—the eminent Welsh lexicographer—now the rector of Llanwrin, who held the living from 1862 to 1876.

But we must return to that wonderful man, St. Tydecho, who was very clever at performing miracles. He was rather superior in this line to the majority of the saints of his time. As a proof of his extraordinary power, we would invite the tourist to accompany us in the direction of the source of the Dovey. Some two miles and a half above Llanymawddwy, in the direction stated, and near Rhiw'r March, may be found what is called "Gwely Tydecho" (Tydecho's Bed)—a mere shelf in the rock. Here Tydecho—for want of better furniture—took his rest. And near this hard bed, a little higher up, is what is called "Buches Tydecho" (Tydecho's Milking Fold). One morning, his maid, returning from milking, had to cross the river, and in doing so her foot slipped, upsetting the milk into the water. Tydecho, instead of chiding his maid, as most Welsh farmers would have done, turned the accident to a good account. He changed the whole river from its source almost as far as the village of Llanymawddwy into a beautiful stream of flowing milk, sweet and creamy; and gave that part of it the name of Llaethnant. It retains the name still. But we must admit that, one day, when we longed to quench our thirst with some of that nutritious liquid, we only found water. However, that was somewhat later than Tydecho's time.

In addition to being the founder of the churches at Llanymawddwy, Mallwyd, Garthbeibio, and Cemmaes, and the innumerable miracles he performed in the shape of giving sight to the blind, hearing to the deaf, and sound limbs to the lame, Tydecho seems to have had spare time to devote to agricultural pursuits. The custom of yoking oxen, instead of horses to the plough, became extinct in this neighbourhood about the beginning of this century. But Tydecho, in addition to oxen, made use of stags to draw the plough, and even tamed wolves were employed to draw the harrow. Wonderful man! But he was not without his troubles. His principal tormentor was the Welsh Chieftain, Maelgwn Gwynedd, who came to steal his cattle. But as the Chieftain was sitting one day on a piece of rock above Ty-nant, in Cwm Llaethnant—probably meditating upon a further plunder—Tydecho, who was busy ploughing on Dol-y-ceirw, caused him, by some supernatural means, to become fixed to his rocky seat. This seat, in a form of a depression in the rock, is still pointed out. The tormentor had to cry for mercy, and was liberated on the promise of abandoning his evil courses, in addition to giving a parcel of land for the benefit of the church.

We do not know whether Tydecho was married, nor, if he was, whether Mrs Tydecho was an amiable wife. However, we are told, that he experienced some trouble on account of his sister, Tegfedd, who, as her name implies, was exceedingly good looking. Her charms attracted the notice of a rich man of the name of Cynon, who fell in love with her—strange to say—against her will, and carried her away by force. Her saintly brother soon overtook them, and the wicked man speedily found out that it was quite useless to play any tricks with Tydecho, who could turn all his calamities into a handsome profit. Cynon had to give up the sister and transfer to the brother, as compensation, some lands for the benefit of the church at Garthbeibio. Here, we may mention, that the church at Llanymawddwy was founded before that of Garthbeibio; and persons from the latter parish on some extraordinary occasions—such as "churching"—used to walk over the mountain to Llanymawddwy. The cairns known as Carneddi'r Gwragedd, on Penygelli mountain, denote the spot where three women met their death by exposure in crossing the hills for this purpose. Therefore Cynon's land was put to a good purpose in providing a site of a church at Garthbeibio, which made such a long and perilous journey unnecessary.

Bala,

A market town 18 miles from Dinas, would be worth visiting to those who like fine rural scenery. It is rather too far for us to enter minutely into its several attractions. However, we may mention the pretty little mound called "Tomen," its Calvinistic Methodists Theological College, and—not to appear bigoted—its new distillery, where Welsh whiskey is manufactured. In our descent from Aran, we indicated the direct road for Bala; that is, by crossing Bwlchygroes for Llanuwchllyn, where we may take the train which conveys us the whole length of Llyn Tegid—a natural lake of about four miles long, and about one mile wide.

Lake Vyrnwy.

We hardly think our tourist will fail to visit this famous reservoir, as the distance from Dinas to the north-west end of it—at Eunant—is only 12 miles. This journey from Dinas to the reservoir, so famous of late years, is more lovely and interesting than the ordinary route from Llanfyllin, and it is superior in all respects to the rough and difficult road of approach from Bala. To reach it, we merely follow the Bala road as far as the summit of Bwlchygroes, and turn along a rough road on our right, which we follow for about three miles. This road, were it not for its wildness, would be very dull; and the last mile of it is spent in descending beside a beautiful, coffee-coloured stream. At last, we turn a corner, and come in sight of the blue, still lake. Our road conducts us to the head of a small bay, where we join the carriage-road, of nearly 12 miles long, which has been constructed round the lake by the Liverpool Corporation.

We cross a picturesque bridge, which spans this arm of the reservoir, with a tall, fantastic crag behind us; and, on turning a corner we see the extent of the lake. It covers the entire bottom of the valley which it has submerged; is rather over five miles long, and varies from three-quarters of a mile to less than a quarter broad; its shape is irregular, following that of the valley. It has all the appearance of a natural lake; entirely surrounded by mountains, which at the top are wild and precipitous, but at the foot are mere pastoral slopes. One mountain behind us juts out into the lake like a wedge, and directs its head into two large bays or horns. Before us—just a mile below where stood the now submerged village of Llanwddyn, with its 35 families—is the picturesque, Rhenish-looking Vyrnwy tower, in which the water is strained before passing into the pipes. Out of the trees above the foot of the lake stands the new, red Hotel; and away at the end, we can see the great arches of the dam. Countless torrents feed the reservoir, many of them forming pretty waterfalls as they fall down the slopes, and are crossed by little bridges from time to time. Nearly four miles from where we touched the lake—we should mention that the top is near Rhiwargor, about a mile to the north—we arrive at the dam, which is a very solid and splendid erection. The work of impounding this sheet of water was commenced in 1881, and the water was stopped by closing the valves of the dam on November 28th, 1888. Among many other interesting particulars found respecting the works in the "Gossiping Guide to Wales," we are informed that this dam is "computed to contain 261,300 cubic yards, some 511 tons in weight. In total height it is 161 feet, but 60 are buried in the foundations; in length it is 1,172 feet; in thickness, at the base it is 120 feet, and the faces of the masonry slope inwards until it becomes a roadway of 20 feet between the parapets. The road is carried on 33 graceful arches across the dam, and through the middle arches the overflow will pour and fall in a cascade nearly 600 feet broad and more than 80 feet high—a superb sight, but not to be seen in very dry weather." The same work goes on to observe that "the estimated storage capacity of the reservoir exceeds 12,000,000,000 gallons, and the daily supply to Liverpool through the single line of pipes first laid down will be more than 13,000,000 gallons, but when the scheme is fully carried out, and three lines of pipe are provided, it will be increased to 40,000,000 gallons, in addition to the compensation water sent down the Vyrnwy, as the Act requires . . . . In length the great aqueduct connecting Vyrnwy with Liverpool exceeds all that have gone before it, being 68¼ miles to the reservoir at Prescot, and 77 miles to the Liverpool Town Hall; and the cost of the works for the first supply of 13,000,000 gallons a day will be about £2,000,000."

The village which supplants drowned Llanwddyn is very ugly; chiefly temporary navvies' huts. The hotel and new church of St. John, with the obelisk erected in memory of those killed in the work, are supposed to be good additions; but are lamentably unpicturesque. The Vyrnwy tower, although admirable in other respects, does not harmonise with the surrounding scenery.

It is an interesting excursion to continue the circuit of the lake from Vyrnwy, along the broad, though somewhat weed-grown, road. The scenery gets very impressive as we get higher up the lake; and, at the very head, near the farm of Rhiw-argor, becomes exceedingly fine. We have dark, precipitous, wooded mountains everywhere; and down a valley, from the direction of Bwlch-y-Pawl, falls the fine cascade of Pistyll-Rhyd-y-Meingciau. The woods round Rhiw-argor are well worth a visit. The road to Bala leads away to the right up to the valley down which was the Vyrnwy; and reaches the old county town after a long and tortuous journey to the mazes of the Berwyns, over Bwlch-Moel-y-Geifr--a bare, steep pass. For wild, bleak scenery, without any distinctive features, this road is unsurpassed. About a mile and a half from Rhiw-argor we come to our original starting point, thus completing the circuit of the lake.

Instead of making this circuitous tour of the lake, the pilgrim may return to Dinas, via Cann Office. To do this he will take the road in a southerly direction from the foot of the reservoir till he gets to the highway near

Llwydiarth. Turning on the right he reaches Cann Office, where again he keeps to the right, passing Garthbeibio and Mallwyd, on his way to Dinas. This circuitous journey may be done by driving, riding, or walking. If the latter, he will probably feel tired, as it is a journey of about 34 miles, made up as follows:—From Dinas to Eunant, 12 miles; from Eunant to the south end of the lake, 4; from there to Cann Office, 6; and from Cann Office to Dinas, 12 miles. The road via Cann Office, over the low pass of Bwlchyfedwen, is smooth and easy walking, but the scenery is not particularly attractive till we come to the last four miles, when we reach Nantyrhedydd, in the neighbourhood where the *Gwylliaid Cochion* were quartered.

To the View of the Seven Valleys

Is a beautiful walk of a short duration, at the end of which we are rewarded by a fine prospect of the surrounding valleys. We may reach it either by taking the wooden bridge from Dolybont Common near the Red Lion, and following the path through the plantation from Tanybwlch; or by taking the road in the direction of Mallwyd; and after leaving Dolbrawdmaeth—the residence of Dr Cocksedge—on the right till we come to a lane close to an outbuilding on our left. Following this lane we gradually wind up the hillside till we reach the Bwlch farm, then turning our face northwards we come to the top of Cyttir, which word, by the way, means *Common Land.* Beneath our feet, running eastward, lies the *valley of Llanymawddwy*, with the Bwlchygroes precipice in the distance. On our left lies the boat-shaped *Cwm Cowarch*, with the summit of the Aran peeping over the northern corner. On the other side of Moel Benddin, *Cwm Cerist* is laid open; with just a peep at the entrance of *Cwm Maesglasau*, and a faint glimpse of Cader Idris through the opening of Bwlchoerddrws. The village of Dinas, at the head of the *Dovey Valley*, lies to our west, and a little below the view of the valley is interrupted by Cefncoch, but comes in sight again below Mallwyd, with the Cemmaes hills forming the foreground of the *Plynlimon* range. Without moving, the eye may scan *Cwm Dugoed* which leads in the direction of Cann Office; and to complete the seven valleys which may be seen from this spot, *Cwm Cewydd* is prevented from joining the vale of Llan-y-mawddwy by the ridge we are standing upon. The views which present themselves from this elevation are almost unparalled, and the eyes of the poet would never tire in surveying them. We may descend from Bwlch farm to Cwm Cewydd, and, taking the road to our right at the little hamlet of the same name and crossing a stile after some five minutes walk, we arrive at Pen-y-braich, which affords another fine view of the Dovey Valley and the village of Dinas.

Mallwyd Church

(1½ mile from Dinas) deserves a visit other than for devotional purposes. It is by no means an imposing edifice; but, as it is, we may be certain that it excels the building put up here by St Tydecho in the sixth century. On entering the Churchyard we are struck by the appearance of an exceedingly large yew tree which stands in the south-east corner. The trunk measures about 27 feet in circumference; and is divided, about five feet from its base, into six thick branches; its height is about 40 feet; whilst the circumference of the ground covered by its branches is about 240 feet. We have heard it suggested, considering the slow growth of this species of trees, that it is not improbable that this particular tree may have been planted as early as Tydecho's time. This supposition, to some extent, is confirmed by examining another yew that grows in the eastern corner. The trunk measures 7 feet 8 inches; and a small stone is fixed at the base with D.E.O., 1613, engraved upon it. And, if that refers to the person who planted it and the time it was done, we may reasonably allow several centuries more for the growth of the large yew at the other corner.

Turning our attention to the Church steeple we find on the south-east of it the words "Solidko Sacrum Christi

MDCXI," rudely made by perforating holes with an augur in the wood-work. The words "VENITI CANTEM," which were to be seen on the north-west side a few years ago, are now almost obliterated. The above date undoubtedly refers to the restoration of the building by the then incumbent—the Rev John Davies, D.D., who was the rector of the parish from 1604 till his death in 1644. It was during his time that two of the three bells were put up in the belfry—the precise date being June 29th, 1639. And from the inscription—C. 1641 H." cut in the woodwork above the porch, we conclude that that part was added then. Were we learned in the science of Palæontology we might be able to say what are the bones which are suspended over the porch. If tradition is to be credited, they are the rib and part of the spine of a whale which was caught in the Dovey in the olden times! But in spite of our veneration for tradition, we cannot swallow the whale story. Whenever and wherever they came from, it seems they were suspended, as they are now, in the year 1816; because they are mentioned by Pugh in his "Cambria Depicta," published that year. Mr Pugh also mentions that the communion table had remained in the centre of the building since Dr. Davies's time, who insisted on having it there in spite of Archbishop Laud's injunction to remove it to the east end. However, the table was removed to the east end in 1853-4, when the building went under a considerable alteration and repair, and when the stained-glass window was put up by the communion table. It will be seen that the walls are decorated with several memorial tablets. But we shall content ourselves by quoting the translation of the Latin tablet on the western wall, which appeared in the *Cambrian Journal* for 1863 :—

Here is Buried
JOHN DAVIES, D.D.,
Born at Llanferres,
In the County of Denbigh,
Rector of this Church for 30 years.

A man of varied literary acquirements,
An earnest defender of religion undefiled,
Remarkably distinguished for the love of his country,
The uprightness of his character recommended him
To two successive Bishops of his own time,
And his learning in Greek, in Latin, and in Hebrew

rendered him to each an useful assistant
in the Welsh translation of the Holy Scriptures.
Also as an able and unbiassed explorer
of the language and Antiquities of Britain,
He laid open her annals long neglected,
And in more than one work paved the way for posterity
To a scientific acquaintance with their ancient tongue,
He died upwards of 70 years old in the year of our Lord 1644.
His Countrymen having raised a subscription 200 years
afterwards,
That the ashes and memory of one who had deserved so well of
his country
might no longer be without a monument,
caused this memorial to be erected
in token of honour and affection.

Dr. JOHN DAVIES, in addition to being an excellent scholar and an author, was also, like many parsons of his time, an expert conjurer. The folk-lorist will pardon us for relating one or two traditions to show his familiarity with the sable gentleman, whose name we need not mention. Being the incumbent of Llanymawddwy as well as Mallwyd, his services on one occasion were solicited somewhere in the former parish to lay down a ghost which had become very troublesome. In those days, conjurers used to cork up spirits in bottles—which process is reversed by modern tipplers, who are too prone to pour out the spirits. On this occasion, after confining the spirit for a certain period, the Doctor went home leaving his conjuring-book behind him in a fit of forgetfulness, and sent his servant for it. This servant—being about one-fifth of a conjurer himself—when he came somewhere about the place where the Railway Station now stands, opened the book and began to read. As soon as he did so a frightful being appeared suddenly before him, and demanded, that in-as-much as he had been called up from the infernal regions, he should have some work to do. The servant had sufficient presence of mind to order him to make a rope of the water of the river; and the evil spirit immediately obeyed. The servant then read on in order to get rid of his unwelcome visitor; but, instead of that, another appeared. When he demanded work, he was told to hinder the other from making the rope. A fearful conflict ensued, and they fought like the very devils, as they were. They kept on fighting till an unusual thunderstorm was produced; and then the Doctor guessing what had occurred, went to meet the servant. He reprimanded him for meddling with things he did not understand, sent the demons to their customary abode, and peace and calm were restored.

On another occasion, Dr. Davies and his servant had occasion to cross the river Dovey, when the river was flooded, and when bridges were not so common as they are now. The reverend Doctor pointed to a fine-looking horse grazing in a field close by, and ordered his man to fetch it They both mounted; but before they were much more than half way over, the servant uttered the name of God, and the horse vanished, leaving them to scramble to dry land as well as they could. The extraordinary behaviour of the horse gives a clue to its pedigree; and we may reasonably assume that this sudden immersion was the cause of turning the Doctor's attention to bridge making.

At any rate, it was through Dr. Davies's means that three bridges were constructed in the neighbourhood. The first of his bridges is MALLWYD BRIDGE, which spans the Dovey on the old road opposite Mallwyd, and just below the weir. This was erected in 1633, and is in good repair at the present time. The second is the old bridge situated a few yards below FFINANT BRIDGE, by the Railway Station, which was erected in 1635. And the third is situated below CLEIFION BRIDGE—between Dinas and Mallwyd—and was put up in 1637. Above the Cleifion Bridge is a pretty little waterfall.

Camlan

Just opposite Mallwyd, on the west side of the Dovey, stands a farm-house called Camlan; and there are other farms on the same side of the river called Maescamlan, Brongamlan, and Camlan Isaf. A modern Welsh writer suggests, on the strength of these place-names, but in opposition to the general opinion, that the Battle of Camlan, in which the renowned King Arthur is said to have fallen, was fought in this neighbourhood. According to Skene, it was fought in Scotland, whilst Camden, Leland, and Sharon Turner are in favour of Cornwall.

For ourselves, seeing that the battle is dated as far back as A.D. 537, we cannot be expected to remember anything about it, and we beg to be excused for not expressing an opinion. However, there is a local tradition to the effect that a terrible battle was fought here some time or another; and the place-names of Cleifion Bridge and Bryncleifion—the pretty little residence just above that bridge—are supposed to denote the locality where the wounded were taken to. Against this supposition philologists may observe that "cleifion" is the Welsh word for *sick*, and not for *wounded*.

Gwylliaid Cochion Mawddwy

(The red banditti of Mawddwy).

But if unable to make a satisfactory claim to the battle of Camlan, Dinas Mawddwy can justly boast of having once been the headquarters of that terrible band of robbers called "Gwylliaid Cochion." The founder of this band, according to one Welsh chronicle, was one Owain ab Cadwgan ab Bleddyn, who, for carrying away Nest, the wife of Gerald de Windsor, the Constable of Pembroke Castle, in 1107, had to flee to Ireland. When this Welsh chieftain returned to this country, he brought with him a band of lawless youths, as wicked as himself, and settled in the woods about Dugoed Mawr, some 2½ miles from Dinas, on the Cann Office road. Here they grew in number, being recruited by outlaws and deserters from the army, and probably intermarrying with the original inhabitants. They lived entirely on plunder, and according to Robert Vaughan, a celebrated Welsh antiquary, who flourished in 1592-1666, were never tired of "robbing, burning of houses, and murthering of people, in soe much that being very numerous, they did often drive great droves of cattell somtymes to the number of a hundred and more from one countrey to another at middle day, as in the tyme of warre without feare, shame, pittie, or punishment, to the utter undoing of the poorer sorte." They were so desperate that the inhabitants had to fix scythes and other sharp instruments in their chimneys to prevent the marauders coming down during the night. Scythes have been taken from the chimneys of Dugoed Mawr, and Esgair Adda, near Llanymawddwy, within living memory But at last the time for their extirpation came. Lewis Owen, of Dolgelley, the Vice-Chamberlain of North Wales and Baron of the Exchequer of Carnarvon, was commissioned to apprehend and put to death as many of the band as he possibly could. He accordingly took with him a great company "of talle and lustie men," and on Christmas Eve, 1554, apprehended and put to death above 80 felons and outlaws.

Collfryn (Hill of Execution).

The spot where they are said to have been executed is situated on a field belonging to Collfryn farm, which stands about half a mile, on the right, from the road between Mallwyd and Cann Office, just opposite 'Dugoed Mawr About 150 yards to the south-east of Collfryn farm-house stands a mound measuring about 10 yards high; the circumference at the base being 70 yards, and the circumference at the top being 30 yards. Here, according to tradition, is where the robbers were put to death and buried on the following morning. As the mound is covered by a crop of oak trees of some scores of years' growth, it cannot be seen till we are close upon it.

Llidiart-y-Barwn (The Baron's Gate).

Retracing our steps to the highway, and walking for about a mile in the direction of Cann Office, but about a 100 yards before we get to Nantyrhedydd, we come to a gate, on the right, at the end of an old parish road leading to Llanymawddwy. At this spot, on All Hallows Eve, 1555, when Baron Owen, with a couple of followers, was returning from the Montgomeryshire Assizes, he was waylaid by the survivors of the band, who had cut down trees to barricade his passage. The Baron fought bravely, but the 30 arrows afterwards found in his dead body showed that the contest was unequal. There is a tradition to the effect that when the Baron executed the eighty in the previous year, an old hag, swarthy in complexion and vicious in disposition, went up to the Baron, and, in a whinning tone, begged upon him to spare the life of her youngest son, pleading as an excuse that he was young and not so hardened in guilt as his companions. But when she found that he was inexorable, exposing her chest, she hissed her threat: "These yellow breasts have given suck to those who shall yet wash their hands in thy heart's blood." This vow was fulfilled to the letter. For when the Baron was lying in the agony of death, two of her remaining sons ripped him open and washed their hands in flowing blood. After the Baron's murder, the robbers were completely disbanded—some were captured, and the rest left the country—so that good order was established. Dinas Mawddwy now can claim to be as peaceable and orderly as any place in Wales. The local police constable, who has been stationed here nine years, informs us that he cannot count nine prisoners locked up by him during that time; and most of those were drunken tramps

Llanbrynmair

(9 miles) may be reached by the pretty little dingle—Cwm Tafolog—by Penrhiwcul, on the Mallwyd side of Dugoed Mawr. We enter the *Cwm* by a steep descent which terminates at Bont-y-byllfa, which spans a small brook. After a further walk of about a mile and a half we pass Groesëol farm a little to our left—a path leads from this farm to Llyn-Coch-Hwyad, a lake famous for its trout. However, we understand that it belongs to Sir Watkin Williams Wynn, Bart.; and therefore visitors would do well to arm themselves with the necessary permission to fish in it. The road to Llanbrynmair is rough for the first four miles, when it considerably improves. But it is prettiest at its roughest parts; and the journey back to Dinas may be done by train, viâ Cemmes Road, which is only 5 miles from Llanbrynmair Station.

To Cemmes Road

(7 miles), through Mallwyd—leaving Aberangell on the right—Cwmllinau, and Cemmaes village, would form another

good walk along a fine, level road. And we should not omit to mention the old road, starting at Minllyn School, which follows the right bank of the Dovey, leading through Aberangell and Llanwrin to Machynlleth.

Train Services.

Visitors wishing to spend a day at either Aberystwyth, Aberdovey, Towyn, Barmouth, or any other watering-place on the Welsh coast, may do so with ease. And we are informed that Mr. C. E. Williams, the manager of the Mawddwy Railway, has arranged with Mr. Aslett, the manager of the Cambrian Railways, for through tickets by convenient trains. We have no doubt that the additional facilities will be greatly appreciated not only by visitors staying at Dinas Mawddwy, but also by those staying at Aberystwyth, Barmouth, and other places, who will be enabled to go to Dinas for a day trip. Referring to these new arrangements an influential paper circulating in the district (*The Cambrian News*, March 17, 1893) says:—

"*There is not a more beautiful place in North Wales than Dinas Mawddwy, and the convenient train arrangements made for the next summer season will doubtless cause thousands of visitors from all parts to visit this secluded spot.*"

Postal Information.

Post closes at 5.55 p.m., except in the winter and spring, when the 6.25 p.m. train from Dinas does not run to Cemmes Road; in that case post closes at 3.30 p.m. Delivery commences at 8 a.m. No Sunday post. Telegraph Office (at the Railway Station) opens from 8 a.m. to 8 p.m. on week days; and from 9 a.m. to 10 a.m. on Sundays.

BUCKLEY ARMS HOTEL,

Dinas Mawddwy, Merionethshire.

Dinas Mawddwy is noted for its resemblance to Switzerland.

FIRST-CLASS FAMILY, COMMERCIAL, FISHING, AND TOURIST HOTEL AND WINTER RESIDENCE.

Every convenience. Private Sitting, Bath, and Billiard Rooms. Lawn Tennis. Excellent Fishing—Salmon, Sewin, and Trout—in the river Dovey and other streams. Within one minute of Railway Station and Telegraph Office.

VISITORS will find every comfort and convenience. It is situated in one of the most picturesque and healthy valleys in Wales, and protected from north and east winds. Aran Mawddwy—the next highest mountain to Snowdon range—is ascended from here, and the scenery around unequalled in North Wales. Headquarters of C.T C. Terms moderate.

Visitors wishing a short but at the same time brilliant walk can ascend in 45 minutes from the Hotel to *Y Cyttir*, from which they will see the Seven Valley Panoramic View, which, considering the accessability, is unsurpassed in Wales. Also, Moel Dinas can be ascended from here in an hour, from which also a grand view can be obtained.

Brakes, Cars, etc., will be in readiness at the above Hotel to convey Visitors to the places of interest, at moderate charges.

Distance from Dolgelley 10 miles ; Bala, 18 ; Cann Office, 13 ; Vyrnwy Lake (north-west end), 12 miles ; Cross Foxes Pass, 7 miles ; Bwlchygroes (the most rugged and difficult Pass in Wales), 7 miles.

W. E. LOVEGROVE, Proprietor.

The Minllyn Slate Co.

SLATE QUARRIES,

Dinas Mawddwy, Merionethshire,

MAKERS OF SLATE SLABS

SUITABLE FOR

Billiard Table Beds, Chimney Pieces,

Lavatories, Cisterns, Silos, Steps,

Window Sills, Table Tops, Head Stones, Dairies,

WINE CELLARS,

Meat Safes, Butter and Pastry Slabs, Advertisement Tablets, Electric Fittings, Mangers, Flagging Building Stones,

AND ALL KIND OF

Enamelled Slate Work, &c.

Prices on application.

Gartheiniog Slate & Slab Quarry,

Aberangell, Cemmes, Mont.,

Within 2 Miles of the Aberangell Station on the Mawddwy Railway.

Makers of SLATE SLABS suitable for the manufacture of

Chimney Pieces

etc.

ALSO BEDS OF

Billiard and Bagatelle Tables.

Any description of Slabs cut to order.

These Slabs are of a Blue colour and are especially adapted for the purpose of Enamelling.

Proprietors—

Owens and Mallory.

H. P. JONES,

Ty'nycounant, Dinas Mawddwy,

Dealer in all Bee-keeping Appliances,

BEGS to call attention to his celebrated WELSH HONEY in the comb or extracted. Prices strictly moderate.

May be had at the Hotels or direct from the Producer.

NAG'S HEAD INN,

DINAS MAWDDWY.

Proprietress, MRS. JANE PLATT.

SITUATED in the midst of splendid scenery, close to the River Dovey. Comfortable accommodation for Tourists, who will receive every attention.
WINES AND SPIRITS. BEST BOTTLED STOUT, &c.

Drapery and Grocery Establishment next door,
Under same Management.

Fine assortment of Fancy Goods.
TERMS MODERATE.

Sun Inn, Llanymawddwy,

DINAS MAWDDWY.

(CLOSE TO TORRENT WALK).

Most convenient starting point for Bwlch-y-groes, the most rugged pass in Wales; also for the Llaethnant ascent of Aran Mawddwy.

Comfortable Accommodation for Visitors. Terms Moderate.

Proprietor, EVAN GRIFFITHS.

GREENWICH HOUSE, MAENGWYN STREET,
MACHYNLLETH.

D. H. EVANS,

PRACTICAL WATCH AND CLOCK MAKER,

Jeweller, Silversmith, and Optician.

Cronometers, Repeaters, and all other kinds of Watches Cleaned and carefully repaired. Excellency of workmanship guaranteed.

Guinea Gold Wedding Rings always in stock.

☞ Half-dozen Venetian Tea Spoons presented to every purchaser of a Wedding Ring.

GUIDES.

The services of the following Persons can be obtained at any time upon two days' notice being given, either to the Persons direct or to MR. O. M. NICHOLSON, *the Station Agent at Dinas Mawddwy :—*

DAVID HUMPHREYS, Ty'nyfedw, Cowarch, near Dinas Mawddwy,

Guide to Aran Mawddwy, by Cwm Cowarch route.

WILLIAM HUMPHREYS, Ty'nymaes, Cowarch, near Dinas Mawddwy,

Guide to Aran Mawddwy via Cowarch.

HUGH EVANS, Perthyfelin, Cowarch, near Dinas Mawddwy,

Guide to Aran Mawddwy via Cowarch,

DAVID REES, Llanymawddwy, near Dinas Mawddwy.

Guide to Aran Mawddwy via Llaethnant.

ROWLAND HUGHES, Dinas Mawddwy,

JOHN LEWIS, Minllyn. Dinas Mawddwy,

General Guides to the neighbourhood.

Mawddwy Railway.

(Change at Cemmes Road on the Cambrian Railways.)

CHEAP THROUGH FARES TO DINAS MAWDDWY.

During the Summer Months cheap Week-day Return Tickets are issued from Aberystwyth, Borth, Towyn, Aberdovey, Barmouth and Dolgelley, to

DINAS MAWDDWY

The nearest Railway Station to Aran Mawddwy,

The next highest mountain to the Snowdon range in Wales, it being 2,972 feet in height, the distance from Dinas Mawddwy being only 4 miles to the foot of same; also to LAKE VYRNWY, the distance being 12 miles from the north-west end.

The Railway runs alongside the RIVER DOVEY for some miles, and the well-wooded hills and scenery along the various walks and drives form a very

PICTURESQUE VIEW,

and is considered by competent judges to be unsurpassed by any in Wales.

Special Train Service for July, August, and September.

Time Tables at the Railway Stations.

"We believe that Dinas Mawddwy will be one of the most popular places in the district for Day Trips now that the difficulty of getting there has been removed."—*Cambrian News.*

Cann Office is 12 miles distant; Bala, 18 miles; Vyrnwy Lake (north-west end), 12 miles; Cross Foxes Pass, 5 miles; Bwlchygroes (the most rugged and difficult Pass in Wales), 7 miles; and Dolgelley, 10 miles.

For further particulars and information see Handbills and Time Tables, or apply to the Station Agent, Dinas Mawddwy, or to

CHAS. E. WILLIAMS,

Dinas Mawddwy, R.S.O. Secretary and General Manager.

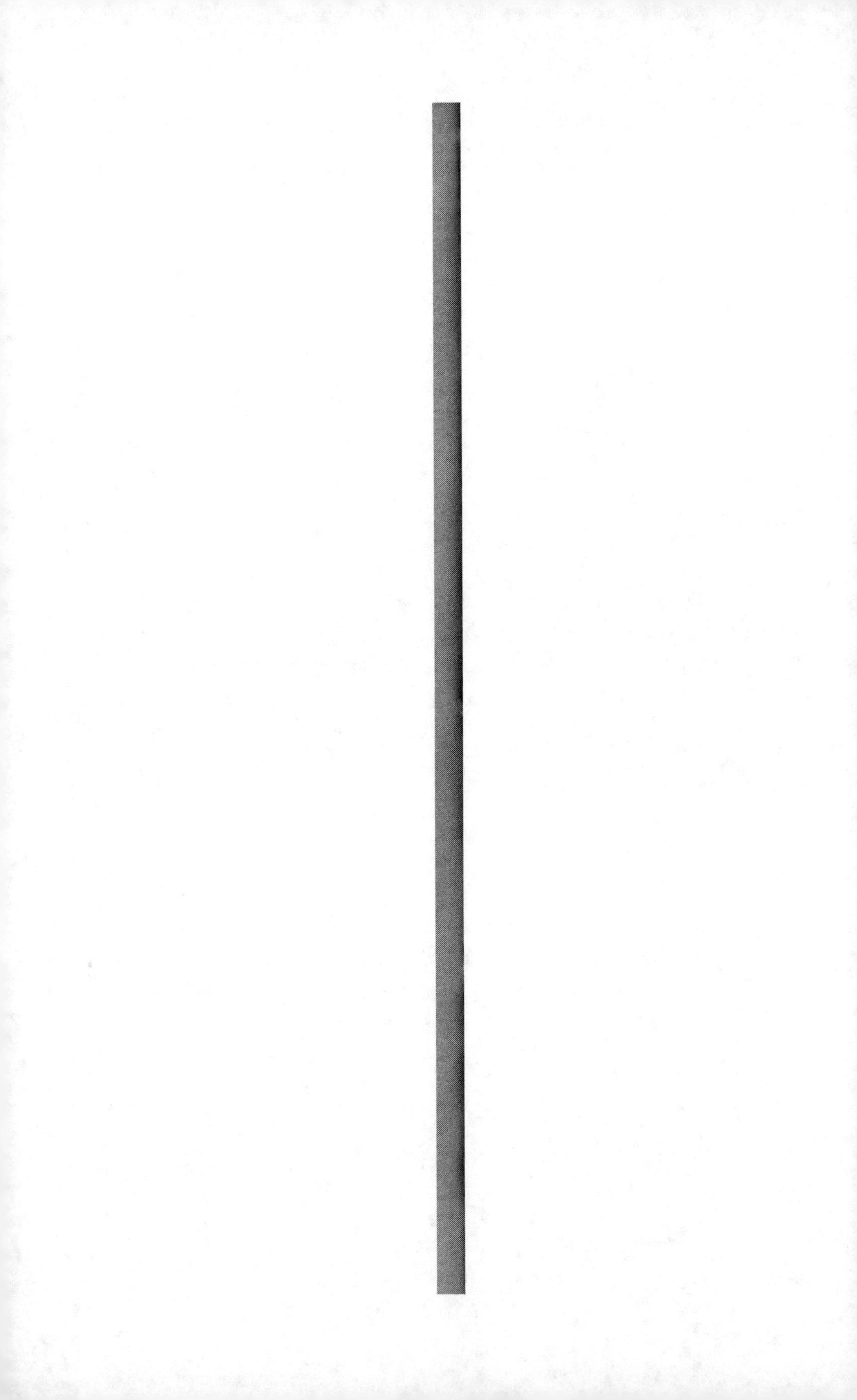

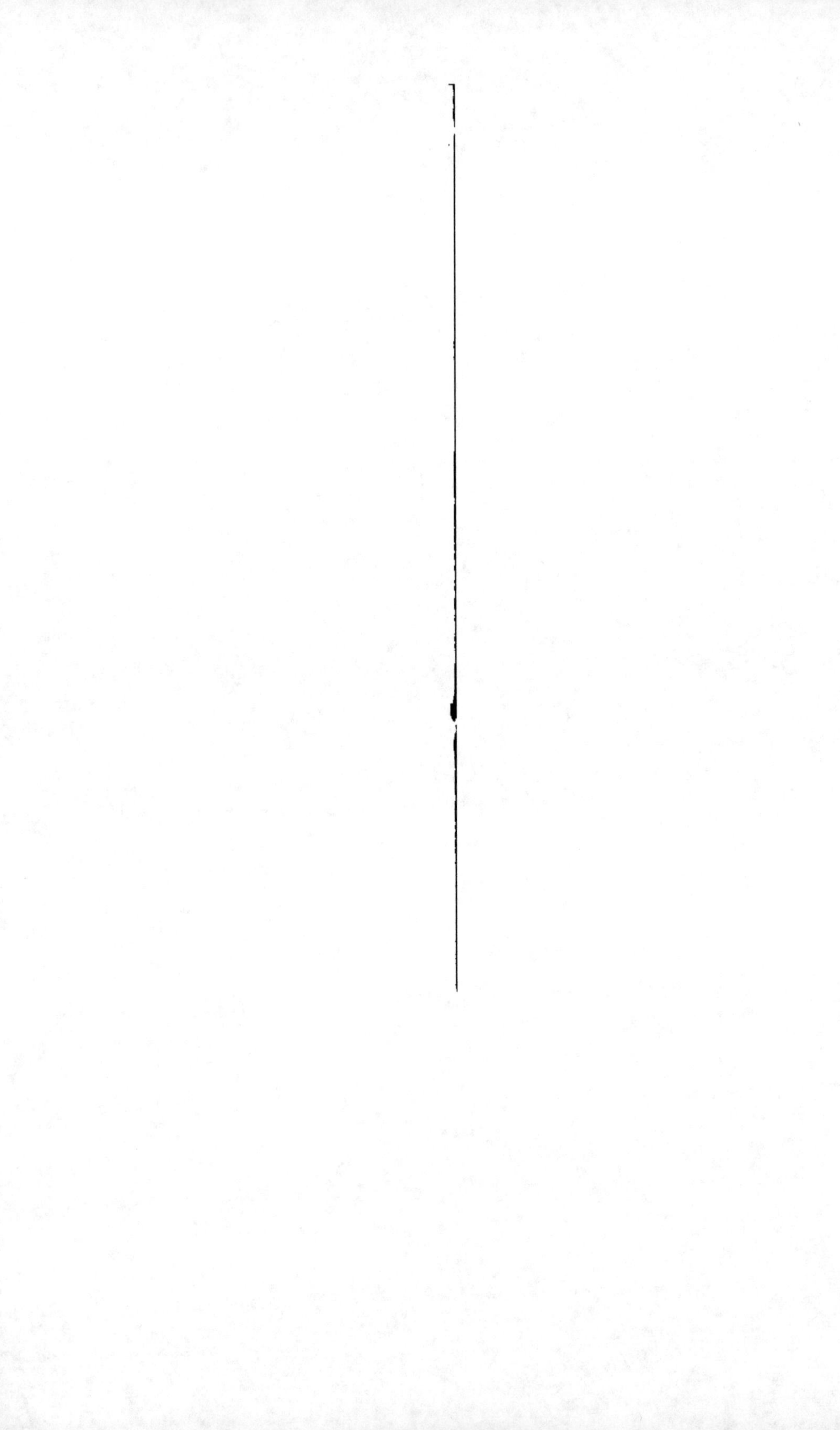

www.ingramcontent.com/pod-product-compliance
Lightning Source LLC
LaVergne TN
LVHW020038170826
845678LV00001B/324

* 9 7 8 0 3 5 3 2 6 6 6 6 7 *